A Book of

by Jillian Po

Contents

Longman

Edinburgh Gate
Harlow, Essex

Human Teeth

Our teeth come in different shapes and sizes. This is because they have different jobs to do. One of their most important jobs is to help us eat.

We have five different types of teeth in our mouth. The sharp pointed teeth are for cutting and tearing food. The wide flat teeth are for grinding and mashing it up.

In the middle at the front we have four top and four bottom teeth. These are called **incisors**. They help cut and chop our food. On either side of them, at the top and at the bottom, we have two pointed teeth. These are called **canine** teeth. They help tear food apart. Next come four teeth at the top and four at the bottom called **premolars**. These teeth help crush our food as we chew it.

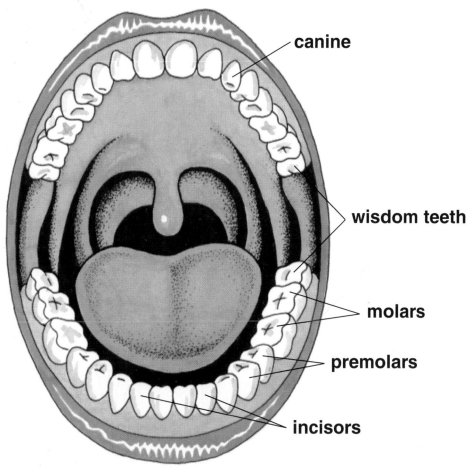

canine

wisdom teeth

molars

premolars

incisors

At the back of our mouths we have four teeth at the top and four at the bottom called **molars**. These are big wide teeth. They work with our tongues to help us swallow food. The tongue takes food to the back of the mouth. Then the molars mash it up until it is ready to be swallowed. Behind them we may grow four **wisdom teeth**, two at the top and two at the bottom. They don't really have a job to do!

We also need our teeth to help us talk. Teeth work with our tongues and lips to help us form speech sounds. This is what happens when we say the word "teeth":

☺ our tongue hits the inside of the top front teeth to say the "t" sound

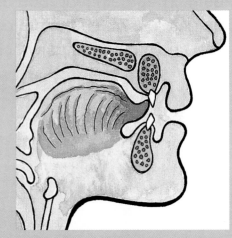

☺ it drops while we make the "ee" sound

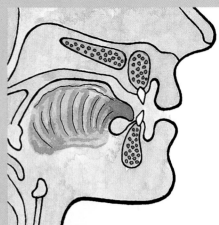

☺ then it goes between the top and bottom teeth to make the "th" sound.

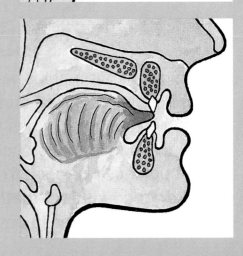

Teeth help give our faces their shape and add to the way we look. We show our teeth when we smile, but people can also show their teeth when they are angry. Teeth can even be used for biting and fighting – or to defend ourselves.

Teeth can help the police identify someone's body after they have died. This is because everyone's teeth are different.

Experts can tell someone's age by looking at their teeth. They can even tell if someone had a job that wore their teeth down – like a musician who played a wind instrument, or a carpenter who held nails between his teeth while he was working.

POSTMORTEM DENTAL RECORD FORM

Identification number _____

Examiners _____

Date _____

RESTORATIONS AND MISSING TEETH

Prosthetic appliances _____

_____

_____

_____

_____

_____

_____

DISEASES AND ABNORMALITIES

Estimated age _____

Sex _____

Race _____

Remarks _____

_____

_____

_____

_____

Animal Teeth

Animals have different kinds of teeth to go with the kind of food they eat.

Meat-eaters like cats and sharks have sharp, pointed teeth. These are for killing their **prey** and tearing raw meat.

Plant-eaters like cows and gorillas have square flat teeth. These are used to grind or mash up grass or vegetables.

Animals that eat both meat and plant foods (like us) have sharp teeth in the front and flat teeth at the back.

Giraffes have 32 teeth – the same number as we do. Some types of whale have only one large tooth. Snails have up to 25 000 teeth. Dinosaurs had nearly 1000 teeth.

Fact

Some dinosaur teeth were up to 30 centimetres long.

If dinosaurs lost a tooth, they could just grow a new one. Sharks lose teeth every week of their lives, and keep growing new ones. They can grow over 20 000 teeth in a lifetime. **Rodents** such as rats, mice and squirrels have front teeth that keep growing. They bite on wood, plastic or metal to keep their teeth sharp and to stop them growing too long.

Animals use their teeth in many different ways. Baboons and monkeys show their teeth when they are angry or frightened. Pigs use their teeth to dig in the ground for roots to eat. Wart hogs and boars have very long teeth that turn upwards. They use them as weapons. Snowshoe rabbits also use their teeth to fight with. Poisonous snakes have hollow **fangs** that can inject poison into their prey or enemy.

Elephant and walrus tusks are a kind of tooth. Walruses use their tusks to dig up food from the seabed. They also use them to defend themselves against enemies like polar bears. Male walruses use their teeth to fight each other when they are looking for a mate.

Elephant tusks are the longest teeth in the world. Elephants do not use them for eating. They are to help them dig up food from the ground or break branches off trees. They also use their tusks to attack enemies or defend themselves and their young.

How Teeth Grow

Fact

- Your teeth contain the hardest substance in your body: enamel.

- Your body has its own superglue for holding teeth in the jawbone.

Babies have "tooth buds" even before they are born. Their baby teeth begin to appear when they are about six or seven months old. We say a baby is "teething" when its teeth are growing.

By the age of three, most children have all their baby teeth – 20 of them. When they are five or six years old, the baby teeth begin to fall out. Usually the top two at the front fall out first. As each tooth falls out, a bigger permanent tooth grows to take its place. Most children have 28 permanent teeth by the age of 14. In the next few years, four more "wisdom" teeth may grow at the back of their mouths to make a full set of 32. Sometimes there isn't room for these teeth so they don't grow through properly.

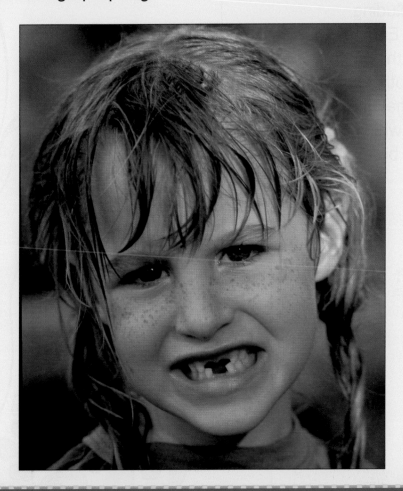

Fact

■ **The teeth in our mouths have** evolved **from bony skin plates that fish once had.**

The structure of teeth

Each tooth has a crown and root. The crown is the part you see growing out of the gum. The root is the hidden part that holds the tooth in the jawbone. The crown is covered in hard shiny **enamel**.

Enamel is the hardest substance in the body. It is made from mineral salts, including calcium. Enamel protects the surface of the tooth. Under the enamel is dentine, which is a bit like bone.

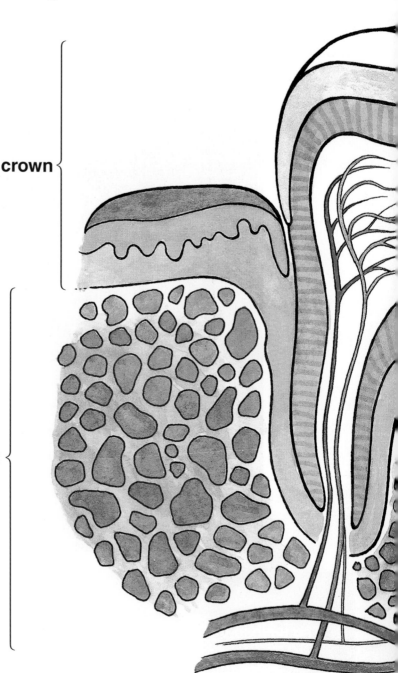

crown

root

Dentine protects the pulp. This is the inside part of the tooth. It contains the tooth's nerve endings. These send messages to the brain if the tooth hurts. It also contains blood vessels that feed the tooth and keep it alive and healthy.

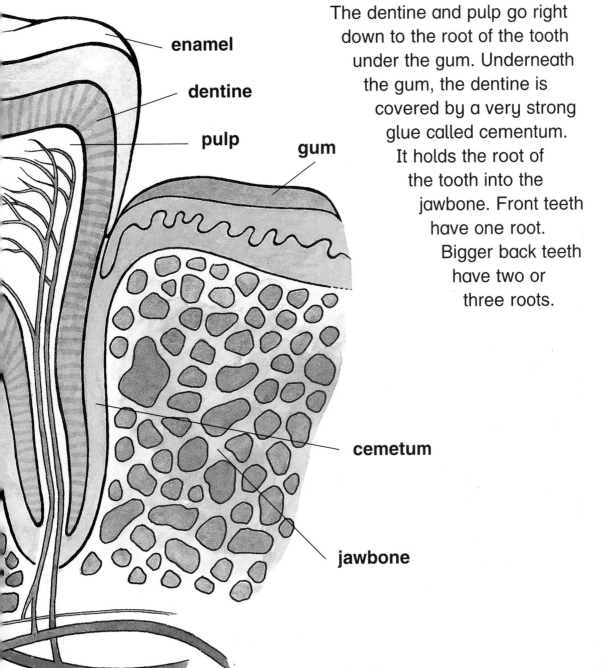

The dentine and pulp go right down to the root of the tooth under the gum. Underneath the gum, the dentine is covered by a very strong glue called cementum. It holds the root of the tooth into the jawbone. Front teeth have one root. Bigger back teeth have two or three roots.

enamel

dentine

pulp

gum

cemetum

jawbone

Tooth Care and Repair

Teeth are the only parts of the body that can't repair themselves. We must look after them properly to help them last us a lifetime.

Keeping teeth and gums clean is an important part of tooth care. We need to brush our teeth at least twice a day, in the morning and at night. The proper way to brush is up and down, not from side to side. We must also remember to clean behind the teeth, too. After brushing, it is a good idea to use dental floss to clean between the teeth, where bits of food can get stuck.

Eating a healthy diet helps keep our teeth strong. Teeth need plenty of calcium, from foods like milk, cheese and yoghurt. Crunchy foods like apples and celery are also good for our teeth. Fresh fruit and vegetables give us the vitamins we need to keep our gums healthy.

We can help our teeth by not having too many sugary foods or drinks. Sugar can damage the enamel and dentine on our teeth. This leads to tooth decay and **cavities**. It is because tiny germs in our mouths change sugar into acids. The germs and acids join together to form a sticky **plaque** that covers the teeth. If we don't clean our teeth properly, plaque starts to eat into the enamel. A cavity can form in the tooth and the tooth starts to decay.

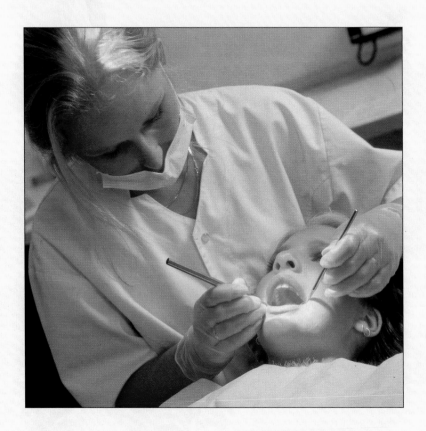

We need to visit a dentist twice a year to check that our teeth and gums are healthy. The dentist may suggest tablets or toothpaste containing **fluoride**, as this helps make the teeth stronger. Teeth can also be coated with fluoride gel or foam to protect them against germs. In some towns and cities, fluoride is added to drinking water to help keep people's teeth strong.

If any teeth are causing pain, the dentist may use X-ray to check if there is any decay or cavities.

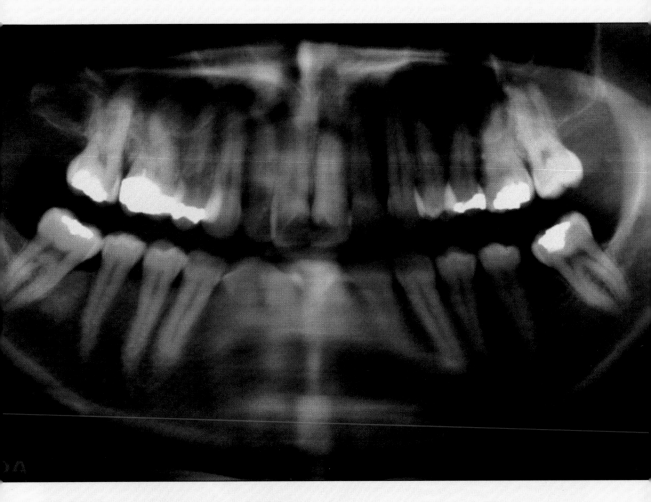

An x-ray showing teeth with fillings

If a cavity has formed, the rotten part is drilled out and replaced with a filling. Fillings can be made from metal or very strong plastic. A tooth that is broken or weak can be fitted with a cap called a crown.

Some people have **cosmetic dentistry** to make their teeth straighter, whiter or more even.

Fact

■ In parts of Asia, people decorate their teeth by chipping or filing them and painting them different colours. In Indonesia, young people have their teeth filed to show that they are leaving childhood behind.

Tooth Care in the Past

Hundreds of years ago, people thought it was a tooth worm that caused tooth decay. Bad teeth were just pulled out. In China, tooth pullers used their fingers. They practised by pulling nails out of planks of wood for up to six hours a day.

In England in the **Middle Ages**, barbers were the people who pulled teeth. They hung the teeth they had pulled outside the shop by their barbers' poles. Even rich people had teeth missing. Queen Elizabeth I hid the gaps in her teeth with bits of cloth when she went out.

Fact

- An Ancient Egyptian cure for toothache was to place a warm split mouse over the jaw.

- Up until the late 1700s, tooth-pullers were entertainers. In Paris, Le Grand Thomas drew huge crowds to watch him pull out bad teeth.

The first toothbrushes were simply twigs frayed at one end. People also used bits of cloth or sponge, or just their fingers, to clean their teeth. The Chinese invented toothbrushes made with animal hair and these were used in Europe by the 1600s.

Fact

- Toothpicks have been found in ancient Chinese and Roman ruins.

- The Roman writer Pliny (23–79 AD) wrote: "It makes teeth firm to pick them with a porcupine quill."

- Ancient writings speak of a toothbrush twig in use over 2500 years ago.

Ancient recipes for tooth powders include dried fruit and flowers, snail shells and animal hooves. They even list ingredients like mice, the head of a hare, lizard livers and urine! Rich Roman women paid for urine from Spain and Portugal because they believed it helped make their teeth whiter and their gums stronger. They employed special slaves to clean their teeth.

Powders and pastes were both used in the Middle Ages, though they often wore away the tooth enamel.

From the 1600s, chemists began to sell tooth powder called dentifrice, but poor people could not afford it. They went on cleaning their teeth with salt or soot, using tooth sticks with a rag over one end.

In Victorian times, pink toothpastes with names like cherry, carnation and tomato were popular. Areca nuts, from a type of palm tree, were the favourite flavouring.

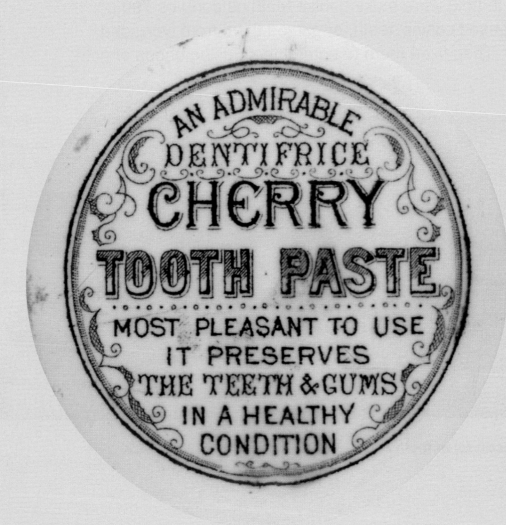

AN ADMIRABLE
DENTIFRICE
CHERRY
TOOTH PASTE
MOST PLEASANT TO USE
IT PRESERVES
THE TEETH & GUMS
IN A HEALTHY
CONDITION

In the twentieth century, toothbrushes were made with nylon rather than hogs' hair. Toothpaste was sold in plastic tubes and pumps, and peppermint became the most popular flavouring.

False Teeth

People began making false teeth over two and a half thousand years ago. We know that the Etruscan people who lived in Italy were making false teeth as early as 700 BC. They used calves' teeth, or carved them from ivory and bone. They fixed them to natural teeth using bands of gold.

Etruscan false teeth

In the Middle Ages, human teeth were used to make false teeth. They were either pulled out of the mouths of dead people, or poor people sold them from their own mouths to get money. The teeth often went brown and smelly. Rich people preferred to have teeth made from silver, gold or mother-of-pearl. False teeth were also carved from elephant or hippopotamus bone, ivory or wood and tied in place with silk.

Fact

■ A collection of nine rotten teeth, from famous mouths like Queen Victoria and Florence Nightingale, was sold to a dentist at an auction in London.

27

In the 1700s, dentists began to use steel springs to hold false teeth in the mouth. The American President George Washington (1732–99) had false teeth made from cows' teeth and metal. Sprung teeth were often badly fitted and had to be removed when the wearer wanted to eat. Sometimes, the springs could make them pop out of the wearer's mouth unexpectedly!

False teeth went brown and smelly after a few months. Fortunately, the first **porcelain** teeth began to be made in the 1770s. These stayed cleaner and whiter. Dentists were also learning how to measure patients' mouths and to make **plaster of paris** moulds so they could fit the false teeth better. By the 1830s, they were using rubber to fix false teeth in the mouth.

A dental plaster of paris cast

Today, false teeth are made from ceramics or plastics. They are light and strong. They can either be taken out each night, or they are fixed in place with a bridge. Teeth can even be fixed into the gum as implants.

Fact

In I993, a Chinese dentist began building a tower of 28 000 bad teeth to make people think about tooth care.

Glossary

canines	pointed teeth
cavities	holes in teeth that have gone bad
cosmetic dentistry	dental work used to improve the look of teeth
enamel	hard material that covers teeth
evolve	to change gradually
fangs	long sharp teeth
fluoride	a chemical that makes teeth stronger
incisors	front teeth used for cutting food
Middle Ages	period in history from about 1000–1500 AD
molars	flat teeth used for grinding and mashing food
plaque	sticky coating that forms on teeth
plaster of paris	a material used to make casts or moulds
porcelain	a type of hard, fine clay
premolars	the teeth just in front of the molars
prey	an animal hunted and killed for food by another animal
rodents	small mammals with large front teeth, e.g. squirrels and rabbits
wisdom teeth	teeth that grow at the back of the mouth